# Four Friends Find Fun
## Discussion Guide

Written by V. L. Doyle and Dr. Robert A. Rohm
with Rebecca Sharp Colmer

Illustrated by Timothy Zulewski

# Four Friends Find Fun
## Discussion Guide

Written by V. L. Doyle and Dr. Robert A. Rohm
with Rebecca Sharp Colmer

Illustrated by Timothy Zulewski

Published by Personality Insights, Inc.
And EKLEKTIKA Press, Inc.

ISBN: 0-9651672-6-7
LCCN: 2004095470


10 9 8 7 6 5 4 3 2 1
First Edition September 2004

Visit www.personalityinsights.com
www.fourfriends.org
www.DrRohm.com

## How to Use This Guide

This booklet guides you, step-by-step, through each page of *Four Friends Find Fun*. It has a simple structure designed to encourage you to lead a discussion about different personality styles. There is a section on each page to record your questions, observations and insights.

## Objectives

This guidebook is to be used as a reference for presenting personality-style concepts featured in *Four Friends Find Fun*. We provide personal insights for personality development, enhanced interaction, and building more effective groups and teams. This approach affirms and enlightens the child to expand on his/her strengths and minimize his/her struggles. Our goal is to touch each child's life with powerful understanding which will lay the foundation for children to accept one another and appreciate their unique strengths and gifts.

Another objective is to allow students the opportunity to begin using and practicing their new found information about personality styles. Every question in the study guide is designed to help students become more interactive with the book, *Four Friends Find Fun*.

## Other Resources Are Also Available

Please visit us at www.DrRohm.com or www.personalityinsights.com for other resource materials you may want to consider using after you complete this study. You may be interested in allowing your child to complete an online Personality Profile Assessment. You will receive over 40 pages of personal information which will be of great benefit to the child, the parent or the teacher. Be sure to check out the online Personality Profile Assessment today!

- Take a closer look at the wallpaper on the inside front and back covers.
- Point out the different symbols: an exclamation point (green), a star (red), a plus and minus sign (blue) and a question mark (yellow).

 D — Exclamation Point — D's are emphatic in everything they do.

 I — Star — I's love recognition and to be the center of attention…and the star of the show.

 S — Plus and Minus Sign — S's have a "more or less" attitude. They are flexible and can go "either way".

 C — Question Mark — C's want to know the "why" behind everything they do.

- Follow the bunny and turn the page.

- Read aloud the title.
- Meet Carl. He is in a yellow truck pulling a camper known for quality.
- Look closely at the emblem on the front panel of the truck. Do you see the question mark? It is the symbol for the "C" personality style.
- Carl is cautious and safety conscious. He is neat and organized.

Notes: _____

_____

_____

_____

_____

_____

_____

Illustrated by Timothy Zulewski.

ISBN: 0-9741760-1-X

Co-published: RS Colmer, EKLEKTIKA Press: 0-9651672-4-0
LCCN: 2004092902

10 9 8 7 6 5 4 3 2    First Printing 2004
Printed in China.

Visit www.personalityinsights.com
www.fourfriends.org

- Meet Sofia. She is in the back seat of a blue van with her luggage on top.
- Point out the emblems on the wheels and luggage rack.
- Sofia likes to help people. She is shy, stable and steady.
- She enjoys the outdoors and nature.
- Point out other details that may be of interest to your child.
- Where do you think they are going?

Notes: _____

_____

_____

_____

_____

_____

6

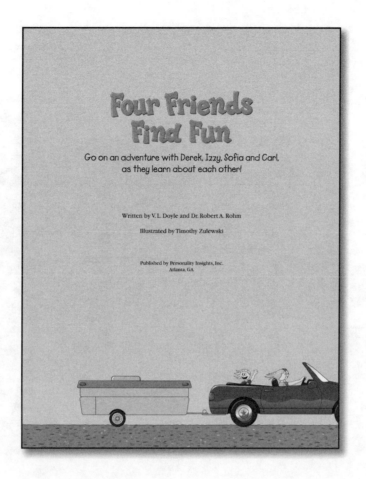

- Read aloud the title and subtitle.
- Meet Izzy. She is in a red convertible. She likes to be seen.
- Point out the stars on the hub caps.
- Izzy is happy and likes to have fun.
- Izzy treats every person she meets like they are her new best friend in the whole world!

Notes: _____

_____

_____

_____

_____

_____

Four little friends named Derek, Izzy, Sofia and Carl, all arrived at camp on the same day.

Once upon a time, deep in the forest, there was a wonderful campground called Camp Augusta. It was the best place in the entire world. It was FULL of fun!

- Read aloud.
- Derek is in a big motor-home. Where is the emblem? (side panel)
- Derek likes to be the best. Derek likes to get results.
- Find all of the different animals in the forest.
- Find the people in the picture. What is each one doing?

Notes: _____

_____

_____

_____

_____

_____

Dynamic Derek was determined to be the first one to start the summer fun. He wanted to set the pace for all of the activities at camp.

! Read aloud.
! Notice that Derek is ready to have fun. He loves to be active and do tasks. The fire pit is ready. He has firewood.
! He plays with his dog. What would be a good name for his dog? Do you have a dog? What is your dog's name?
! Derek is active and likes to keep moving. He is outgoing.
! Derek has a lot of energy and plays real hard.

Notes: _____

_____

_____

_____

_____

_____

Inspiring Izzy could not stop talking about how excited she was!
She had been dreaming of this day since last summer.

★ Read aloud.
★ Look at Izzy. She is outgoing, too.  She is excited to be camping. She likes to be the center of attention.
★ Notice there is only one sandal in the picture.  The other one may be in her suitcase or who knows where! Izzy is messy, look at her suitcase. She is like a tornado!
★ Izzy likes bright colors.
★ Izzy is more interested in people than performing tasks. She has a difficult time staying focused on anything for very long.
★ Izzy has a lot of energy.

Notes: _____
_____
_____
_____

Sweet Sofia made treats for all of her friends.
She liked to make everyone feel special.

± Read aloud.
± Sofia wants everyone to feel welcome and happy.
± She has a welcome mat in front of her tent. Notice her diary. She likes to remember special things.
± She is quiet and reserved.
± Sofia normally likes to be with just one or two people at a time. She sometimes feels overwhelmed in a large crowd.

Notes: _____

_____

_____

_____

_____

_____

Cautious Carl wanted to have the perfect campsite –
orderly, neat and clean. He even set up his telescope
for studying the stars later that night.

? Read aloud.

? Carl is planning. Notice the reference books.

? He has a first aid kit and a telescope.

? He labels everything. He is well prepared.

? He is reserved, too. Carl does not mind working alone.

Notes: _____

_____

_____

_____

_____

_____

- Read aloud. This is called the "dream page".
- Has anyone noticed the bunny in most of the pictures?
! Look at Derek. He is not afraid. He is ready to find a ghost and go get him!
★ Izzy does not like to be alone. She likes to be with her friends.
± Sofia is worried that something bad may happen. A lot of things scare her.
? Carl has a detailed dream and story. He has a vivid imagination.

Notes: _____

_____

_____

_____

_____

_____

13

- Read aloud.
! Derek is standing up. He likes to tell people what to do. Most of the time he believes he is in charge.
★ Izzy uses her hands and facial features to communicate. She likes to tell stories but sometimes loses track of time.
± Sofia burns her marshmallow because she is so engrossed in watching Derek and Izzy. She brought her purple pillow to sit on to be comfortable.
? Carl sits up straight. He is a good listener. He is prepared. Notice the canteen and flashlight. He is thinking.

Notes: _____

_____

_____

_____

_____

The next morning, the four friends met at the boat dock. They were going fishing!

Derek was the captain of the boat. He liked to be in charge, and he was a quick decision maker.

- Read aloud.
! Derek is ready to go. He is not wearing a life preserver. He is already in the boat, but not really prepared. All he has with him is what he thinks he needs.
★ Izzy is running. She does not even notice the "No Running" sign. She likes having fun and does not notice she could be in danger. Have you ever acted like Izzy?
± Sofia has a picnic basket. She is caring and thoughtful. She walks slowly and is very calm.
? Carl is well prepared. He is carrying all of the safety items that he and his friends might need.

Notes:
_____
_____
_____
_____
_____

15

★ Read aloud.

★ Izzy has gummy worms in her hand. The gummy worms are very colorful. Unfortunately, fish do not like gummy worms!

★ She has stars on her bathing suit.

★ She jumps into the boat. She is not the cautious type.

Notes: _____

_____

_____

_____

_____

_____

Sofia wanted everyone to be safe.
She liked to know what to expect ahead of time.
She was feeling a little fearful about the adventure.

± Read aloud.

± Sofia is holding on to the rail. She is not sure about this adventure.

± She is worried that Izzy is not being safe.

± Although Sofia really loves and enjoys her friends, she knows there is always the possibility that things could go wrong.

Notes: _____

_____

_____

_____

_____

Carl was very organized. He reviewed his checklist one more time and then gave everyone a life preserver. He liked to be prepared.

? Read aloud.

? What has Carl brought with him? (sun block, first-aid kit, life jackets, etc.)

? Carl checks things off his list.

? He is prepared. He is safety conscious.

Notes: _____

_____

_____

_____

_____

_____

- Read aloud.
- Notice how each person compliments the other.
! Derek keeps things moving. He likes to be the leader.
★ Izzy makes the trip fun. She likes to sing and make noise.
± Sofia keeps things steady. She likes for things to be calm and quiet.
? Carl follows the directions and the map. He is busy doing tasks.

Notes: _____

_____

_____

_____

_____

_____

- Read aloud.
- As soon as Izzy catches a fish, Derek takes over.
- Sofia notices the dark clouds, but does not speak up or say anything. She is frozen in fear.
- Carl cannot get their attention about the approaching danger.
- What are the fish doing?

Notes: _____

_____

_____

_____

_____

_____

- Read aloud.
- ? Carl looks ahead and sees the waterfall but cannot get anyone's attention.
- ± Sofia's comfort level is being challenged. She is getting nervous.
- ★ Izzy is still excited and does not notice her surroundings.
- ! Derek wants to be the hero. He is focused on reeling in the big catch.

Notes: _____

_____

_____

_____

_____

_____

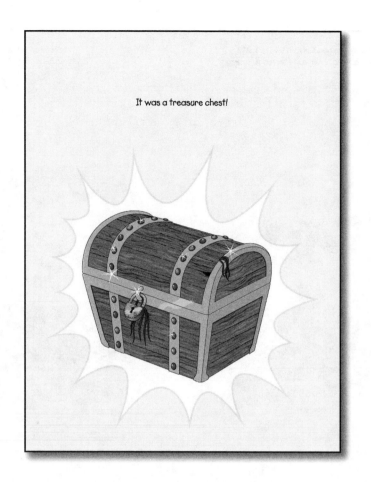

It was a treasure chest!

- Read aloud
- Try to guess what is in the treasure chest. (Listen carefully to the guesses from the students/children.)

Notes: _____

_____

_____

_____

_____

_____

_____

_____

_____

- Read aloud
- ! Derek is intent on getting the chest open. He is still in charge!
- ★ Izzy is so excited!
- ± Sofia is hanging on. She is uncomfortable and unsure about what might happen next.
- ? Carl knows the waterfall is ahead of them. He wants to be safe.

Notes: _____

_____

_____

_____

_____

_____

The kids screamed as their boat went over the waterfall and flipped upside down. The treasure chest was lost. They swam to shore and ran to their campsites to get out of the storm.

- • Read aloud
- ! Derek is first to get to shore.
- ★ Izzy is taking it all in stride.
- ± Sofia is in a panic.
- ? Carl is surprised and shocked that Derek let it all happen.
- • What do you think the bunny is thinking to himself?

Notes: _____

_____

_____

_____

_____

_____

Later that night, the four friends sat around the campfire. Izzy was wiggling with excitement: "We actually had the treasure in our hands," she squealed. Carl asked everyone, "Do you think it was Princess Augusta's treasure?"

"Of course it was, and we are going back out tomorrow to get it," declared Derek. Izzy bubbled over with excitement. Carl knew just where to find the treasure chest. He remembered seeing a willow tree close to where it sank. Sofia whispered, "Maybe we will need some more help."

- Read aloud
! Derek is confident they will go back and be able to find the treasure chest.
★ Izzy is ready for the next adventure.
± Sofia is not sure. She is still a little scared about what has already happened. She thinks they may need some more help.
? Carl is quiet and continues to be a good listener. He has a good memory and remembers details.

Notes: _____

_____

_____

_____

_____

_____

- Read aloud
- Notice how each friend worked together.
! Derek enjoyed leading his friends on an adventure.
★ Izzy enjoyed being with her friends and having fun.
± Sofia enjoyed caring for her friends and trying to help everything run smoothly.
? Carl enjoyed preparing for the trip and actually discovering the treasure.

Notes: _____

_____

_____

_____

_____

_____

**Reader's Guide**

**Derek**
Derek was a dynamic individual who made decisions easily. He was demanding at times and somewhat controlling in his attitude. He often had more confidence than ability.

**Izzy**
Izzy was inspiring and full of energy. Her exciting nature made every event adventuresome and fun. She was the life of the party. Sometimes when she was over-excited, she had a tendency to get into trouble.

**Sofia**
Sofia was sweet and caring. She liked a safe environment in order to stay calm. Although shy at times, she was very thoughtful and considerate of her friends. Sofia had a hard time speaking up when she felt fearful.

**Carl**
Carl was cautious and careful in all he did. He spent time gathering details in order to create a factual plan. His inquisitive and questioning nature helped ensure safety for his friends. Sometimes Carl's concentration on the task at hand caused him to overlook the value found in close relationships.

**1.** Read aloud and discuss.

**2.** Ask each child which character they think is most like themselves and why.

Notes: _____

_____

_____

_____

_____

_____

_____

_____

**3.** Derek and Izzy are fast-paced while Sofia and Carl are slower-paced.

**Activity**:  Sit in a circle. Put everybody that is fast-paced on one side and everybody who is slower-paced on the other side. To help determine each child's style, ask the following questions:
- Who is more like Derek and Izzy?
- Who is more like Sofia and Carl?

Remember, one pace is not better than the other, they are just different.

Notes:
_____
_____
_____
_____
_____
_____
_____

**4.** Get the Picture… The four types are like four parts of a pie. Before seeing the four parts as they stand alone, let's look at the pie in two parts. These two types are different from each other. Think of it this way: some kids are more outgoing like Derek and Izzy, while others are more reserved like Sofia and Carl. There are also two other parts of the pie that are also different from each other. Some kids are more task-oriented, while others are more people-oriented. Task oriented kids like Derek and Carl enjoy doing "things" (directing and correcting) while people-oriented kids like Izzy and Sofia, like to relate with others (interacting and sharing). When you look at the four parts of the pie together, you can visualize the four personality styles. Everyone is a unique blend of these four parts.

**5.** Are you like Derek?

! Derek likes to make decisions quickly.
! When Derek starts a project, he finishes it.
! Derek is confidant.
! Derek gets right to the point when he talks with people.
! Sometimes he gets impatient with people who tell long stories.
! Derek likes to be the leader.
! Derek loves to compete and win.
! Derek likes to do things his own way.

**6.** Are you like Izzy?

★ Izzy likes to talk. She is never at a loss for word

★ Izzy likes being with a group of her friends. Sh
  likes to be the center of attention.

★ Izzy has lots of friends.

★ Izzy is not always as organized as
  she should be.

★ Izzy is very expressive.

★ Izzy can talk people into doing fun things.

★ Izzy tends to jump from one activity to the nex

**7.** Are you like Sofia?

± Sofia likes to help people.

± Sofia is easygoing.

± Sofia is soft-hearted.

± Sofia does not like projects where she is expected to
  figure out how something is to be done. Show her how
  to do it and she will do it well.

± Sofia would rather be a follower than a leader.

± Sofia holds her feelings inside.

± Sofia is good at short-term planning.

**8.** Are you like Carl?

? Carl likes to focus on doing things right.

? Carl is good at organizing

? Carl has respect for rules and authority.

? Carl is a good planner.

? Carl is tactful, diplomatic and courteous.

? Under pressure Carl avoids confrontation.

? Carl does not like to make mistakes.

**9.** Every strength pushed to an extreme or used inappropriately, can become a limitation. As each child discovers his/her personality style, he/she also needs to learn that every strength carries with it, a corresponding limitation.

| | Strength | Corresponding Limitation |
|---|---|---|
| **D** | Goal-oriented | Impatient |
| | Confident | Self-sufficient |
| | Competitive | Attacks first |
| | Determined | Stubborn |
| | Courageous | Reckless |
| | Direct, straightforward | Blunt, tactless |
| | | |
| **I** | Outgoing | Unfocused |
| | Enthusiastic | Excitable, emotional |
| | Good communicator | Talks too much |
| | Optimistic | Unrealistic |
| | Imaginative | Day dreamer |
| | People-person | Disorganized with tasks |
| | | |
| **S** | Stable | Lacks enthusiasm |
| | Steady | Resists change |
| | Easygoing | Indecisive |
| | Agreeable | Over accomodating |
| | Soft-hearted | Easily manipulated |
| | Helpful | Smothering |
| | | |
| **C** | Analytical | Nit-picking |
| | Cautious | Unsociable, suspicious |
| | Conscientious | Worries too much |
| | High personal standards | Judgmental, critical |
| | Strives for excellence | Perfectionistic |
| | Intuitive, sensitive | Easily hurt by criticism |

**10.** Encourage each student to share what he/she thinks might happen next. We want to hear from you. Send us an e-mail: info@DrRohm.com or info@personalityinsights.com.

31